Geoff Thompson's Ground Fighting Series

Fighting From Your Knees

Geoff Thompson

SUMMERSDALE

First published 1996.

This edition copyright © Geoff Thompson 2001

Summersdale Publishers Ltd
46 West Street
Chichester
West Sussex
PO19 1RP
United Kingdom

www.summersdale.com

Printed and bound in Great Britain.

ISBN 1 84024 175 6

Photographs by Paul Raynor

Important note

With ground fighting techniques the author recommends that you practice only under supervision to avoid accidents and always employ the 'tap system' in practice (if you want to submit or a technique is too painful or you wish to stop practice at any time tap the mat, tap yourself or your opponent with your hand or foot; if this is not possible just say to your opponent 'tap'). If an opponent taps out it is imperative that you release your hold immediately or suffer the consequence of what might be serious injury, and remember, what goes around comes around. If you do not release when he taps he may not release the next time you tap.

If you have or believe you may have a medical condition the techniques outlined in this book should not be attempted without first consulting your doctor. Some of the techniques in this book require a high level of fitness and suppleness and should not be attempted by someone lacking such fitness. The author and the publishers cannot accept any responsibility for any proceedings or prosecutions brought or instituted against any person or body as a result of the use or misuse of any techniques described in this book or any loss, injury or damage caused thereby.

About the author

Geoff Thompson has written over 20 published books and is known world wide for his autobiography *Watch My back*, about his nine years working as a night club doorman. He holds the rank of 6th Dan black belt in Japanese karate, 1st Dan in Judo and is also qualified to senior instructor level in various other forms of wrestling and martial arts. He has several scripts for stage, screen and TV in development with Destiny Films.

He has published several articles for GQ magazine, and has also been featured in *FHM*, *Maxim*, *Arena*, *Front* and *Loaded* magazines, and has been featured many times on mainstream TV.

Geoff is currently a contributing editor for *Men's Fitness* magazine.

For full details of other books and videos by

Geoff Thompson, visit www.geoffthompson.com

ACKNOWLEDGEMENTS

With special thanks to Marc McFann and my good friend and grappling sempai Rick Young.

Contents

Introduction

The uninitiated, those that have not got very much real life experience of fighting on the pavement arena and certainly those that have never done any all out grappling, always say 'yea, but . . . I'm never gonna be in this position/that position etc.' And I have to say that it makes me smile because, in a single sentence, they've told me a hell of a lot about themselves. The main thing being that they are not, no matter how much they try to convince you or others, very experienced in things REAL, otherwise they simply would not say it.

Another very common comment is, 'yeah, but surely if you're on your back/side/belly/upside down etc. your have made a grave mistake!'

Yes, it often does mean just that, but we all make mistakes, even monkeys fall out of trees from time to time, but that does not mean that we do not address the problem. Sure, being on your back with the opponent mounting you means you have made a big mistake, but it still has to be addressed because if we make that mistake (I have a few times) we need to know how to deal with it, how to escape it, defend it and even how to attack from it - otherwise when we do meet that situation we won't know how to deal with it.

I remember, early on in my martial arts career, I'd just started working on the doors and realised how close range real fighting was, asking one of my sempais, a man that I did and do greatly admire, 'what do I do if a fight hits the floor, the training we are doing is not preparing me for close range fighting?'

He spent a few seconds in contemplation and then said 'well, if you are on the floor you've made a big mistake - don't let it happen'.

As though a good beating was my just desserts for allowing a situation to go to ground and rather than train to meet that problem I should train to prevent it. I was still left with an unanswered question because, no matter how well or hard I trained I knew that there were going to be times when I would make mistakes and end up in a position that my system

Fighting From Your Knees

did not prepare me for. Eventually I found my own answers to the questions that every one around me seemed to be avoiding, 'we don't fight on the floor', 'don't look at everything from a self defence view point', 'it's not the system that's lacking - it's you, train harder', etc.

And my answer, of course, was firstly to try to avoid negative positions, but also to find solutions, by training in systems that gave the answers to the problems should they occur.

One of the many positions that people think is unlikely to occur in the street (or anywhere for that matter) is fighting from your knees. Again, if you'd 'been there' you'd know that every position is usual when reality bites.

One of my friends, a very experienced street fighter, lost a fight in the toilets of a bar from the kneeling position, but had he known how to fight from his knees he surely would have won. He'd gone to the toilet, as you do after several pints of lager, and was followed by a chap who he recognised as someone from an earlier encounter (a fight a couple of months before). When he got to the trough he undid his zip and pretended to go to the toilet: the guy that followed him in took his chance and grabbed my friend, thinking that he was mid-piss as it were. 'Bosh!' My friend head butted him so hard that the guy was thrown, blood gushing from his nose, right across the toilet floor. This is where my friend made his first mistake. He should have ran in and finished what he had started, but he didn't: he stood back to admire his work.

The guy got back to his feet, ran from the other side of the room and, before my friend could react, he'd been grabbed by the tie and pulled to his knees. They both struggled in the kneeling position for several minutes. My friend's tie was pulled tightly around his neck, cutting off the blood to his brain. He was nearly unconscious - he had no answer to the problem and eventually had to concede before he was completely knocked out. It took him 10 minutes before he could stand back up with out falling over, his assailant wandered off, and as much as my mate wanted to follow and finish him he couldn't, his head was gone. He said to me afterwards, in retrospect, that he was just glad that the lad didn't know that he had a strangle on otherwise he might not be there telling me about the situation.

Fighting From Your Knees

On another occasion I was acting as a second on a square go between two very able fighters, within seconds the fight went to ground and both were on their knees fighting for a prone position but neither had the knowledge to take advantage. At one stage one of the lads got one arm around his opponent's neck whilst he punched him with the other. If he had joined his hands from the position he was in, over his opponent's all fours, he could have made a choke and the fight would have been over by KO within seconds. Instead (because he did not have any knowledge of fighting from that position) he released his partial choke and used his hands to punch instead - the fight went on for several minutes with both fighters getting badly injured. Knowledge of the ground would have made a clinical, one-sided fight out of what turned into an epic battle.

One of the many good things about Animal Day (see my book and videos on *Animal Day*) is that it will teach you all of these things and show you categorically that you do need to be able to fight from every and any angle, otherwise, when you hit the deck you'll be thinking 'what do I do now?' Many people think that by being fit and strong they'll automatically be able to fight on the floor, a bit like saying 'I'm fit and strong, I'll be able to box'. Being fit and strong does not give you the knowledge, and fitness and strength can become redundant commodities if you do not know what to do with them. Having bags full of money doesn't mean that you'll automatically be good on the stock exchange, because money spent unwisely will make you a pauper.

If you're still not convinced then I'll try no more, what I will say is put your money where your mouth is and try it at your own club. Try back to back grappling for 30 minutes and tell me that you didn't end up in every conceivable position on the good God's earth. As my sempai Peter Consterdine is constantly saying, 'feeling is believing'.

The reason I am so emphatic on this subject is that I've been there, many many times and feel that it is my absolute duty as a martial arts writer to tell you 'how it is' so that you do not have to find out like I and so many others of my ilk, the hard way.

Fighting From Your Knees

Fighting on the knees is an important part of ground fighting because one does end up there quite often in a real encounter. This book and the video that accompanies it will give you the knowledge to address it positively when it does.

Review

For those who have read the other volumes in this series I apologise for repeating material. I would like, before I start talking about fighting from the knees, quickly to review the basic pins. If you do not know them a lot of the speak throughout the text may seem like gobble-de-gook.

I have no intention of actually going into the histrionics of the holds, how to defend and how to attack from them etc. that, as I said, is a volume on its own. I will repeat, though, that the pins are the bedrock of ground fighting and to go on to finishing techniques of a complex nature before learning the imperative basics is a quick way to failing at everything that you attempt.

Master the standing and walking before you try the running and sprinting. The control of the opponent on the floor, via the pinning techniques, is so very, very, VERY important that to miss it is like diving in the water before you have learned to swim.

Fighting From Your Knees

All I will list in this chapter is the holds themselves with one accompanying illustration so that, if you haven't read the other books and have no knowledge of the 'ground' you'll at least understand the 'speak'.

The Mount Position

Side Mount

Reverse Mount

Fighting From Your Knees

The Side Four quarter

The Scarf Hold

The Jack-Knife

Reverse Scarf Hold

Fighting From Your Knees

Upper 4 / 14 Pin

Chapter One

Head to head

The head to head position is when you and the opponent are kneeling vertically with heads touching, as per illustration. It can happen at anytime within a conflict, but more specifically when you and the opponent have first fallen (or thrown/been thrown) to the ground or you are already on the ground and either of you is trying to get back to a standing position.

It is a very important position because the knowledgeable fighter may take a strong pin from here that could and probably would determine the outcome of the fight, that fighter needs to be you. Any lack of concentration on your part, from here, could, and will, directly result in you being turned or pushed onto your back from where a strong fighter will take the fight no matter how competent you might be in other ranges or positions.

This is not a great position to strike from because it lacks leverage but striking is still possible and strong enough to

Fighting From Your Knees

cause a reaction which will allow you the initiative to take the opponent over in one of the following holds.

Some of the moves from the head to head position are finishing techniques in themselves, others just lead to better and more potent positions for finishing the opponent.

Striking

Biting

The bite is probably the very best finisher from this position. The ears and nose are most vulnerable.

Butting

This is quite an accessible technique from this position, attacking the side of the opponent's face or his nose and mouth. It may not finish him but it will certainly act as a precursor to a more potent manoeuvre.

Fighting From Your Knees

Punching/Elbowing/Gouging

This is viable if you can get one of your arms free, this is not always easy because the opponent will hold your arms tightly to stop you using them as a weapon, and you'll do the same to him. If you can get a hand free pull it back and attack the opponent's face/jaw/eyes (whatever is most vulnerable at the time) with your fingers, fists and/or elbows. Combining head and hand strikes is also very useful.

Larynx Grab

Again, if you can get one hand free then grabbing the larynx can be a very favourable and effective attack, especially if you have a good grip. It is often not that hard for the opponent to escape from the larynx grab, but in trying to escape he will leave himself wide open for other techniques. I often use the larynx and striking techniques for just that reason, it opens the doors for more potent techniques, having said that they have also been good finishing techniques for me as well.

Lapel choke

This is an excellent finishing technique from any position, the knees being no exception. It can also work very well, as was demonstrated in the true story in the intro to this book, using the opponent's tie to choke him out by simply tightening it until he cannot breath or the blood is stopped to his brain via the carotid artery (at the side of the neck). For the lapel choke, grab the opponent's collar at his right hand side, as deep into the neck as possible, with your right hand, palm up so that your thumb is sticking into his neck. Then grab his opposite lapel, lower down with your left hand, scissor the two hands together to make the choke.

The snatch and turn

Snatch the opponent violently forward by pulling fast on an appendage (the clothes or head will do) so that he is under your all fours, as per illustration. Move around to his side (left or right) simultaneously feeding your right arm under his chin (if going for the face bar feed your right arm across his face so that the bone of the wrist is across his cheek bone, teeth, nose, or eye). Pull him backwards so that he falls between your legs and into your scissor guard, at the same time join your right and left hand to make the choke. As you squeeze your arms to make the choke push down with your feet and stretch the opponent, this will help to secure and tighten the hold.

Fighting From Your Knees

The arm drag

Grip the opponent's right wrist with your left hand, elbow him in the face with your right elbow and bring your right arm-pit onto his right shoulder/biceps and sit forward forcing the opponent onto his back. Keep your back right across his chest to pin him and to stop him reaching for a choke. Reach your right arm behind and around his neck and sit into the scarf hold position.

Fighting From Your Knees

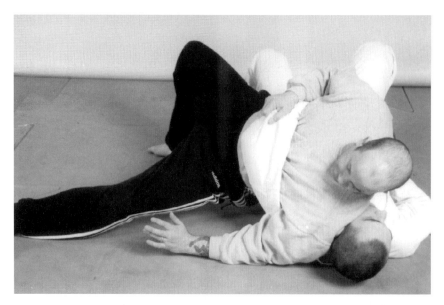

Opposite arm drag

This is more viable when the opponent is grabbing across your body, his right to your right or his left to your left. Grab his right hand with your right hand to keep it in place, elbow him in the face with your left elbow and then drop your left arm-pit across his right shoulder/biceps and force him forward onto his face. You will automatically fall into a shoulder bar, as per illustration.

Fighting From Your Knees

Knee trap and pull

Place your right foot next to the opponent's right knee to stop him spreading his weight and blocking your technique. Pull on his left arm and literally sit down forcing the opponent over onto his back. Roll with him so that you land in the mount position.

Grapevine-knee trap and pull

The same as above only first grapevine your left arm around the opponent's right arm, then trap his knee with your left foot and roll him onto his back, follow into the mount.

Broken choke

Duck under the opponent's right arm and feed your right arm across his neck, couple together to make the strangle and squeeze for effect. If you do not have the leverage to make the choke work, roll the opponent to your left and

climb into the mount, still being sure to hold the strangle. From the mount go onto your toes and focus your weight behind the technique, or alternatively jump into the jack-knife position and strangle from there.

Fighting From Your Knees

The sit and flip

Place your left leg down the right side of the opponent's body and your right leg between his legs. Sit all your weight down and pull the opponent via your grip, at the same time raise your right leg between the opponent's legs and flip him over to your left. As he goes onto his back roll through and find the mount position.

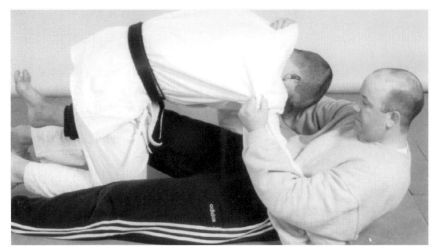

Head lock turn

Whip your right arm around the opponent's head and grab him in a side head lock, pull him over to his own right and force him onto his back, sit into the scarf hold.

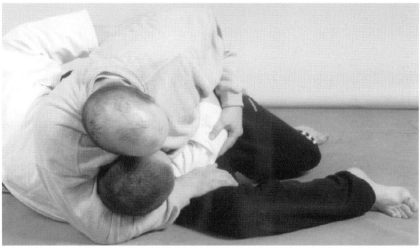

Fighting From Your Knees

Try and formulate your own techniques from the same position, remember there are no rules other than that the technique should work under pressure. As with most techniques these are best taken quickly using the element of surprise before the opponent has a chance to block the move. You don't want to be fighting biceps against biceps, the best techniques are the ones that the opponent gives you.

If you develop the sensitivity that is vital in this arena you will feel his energy and be able to go with it as opposed to against it, that way his strength and power will aid your technique. This can also be accomplished by tricking the opponent by pretending to go for one technique then, just as he adjusts his balance to block the move you take a technique in the direction of his readjusted force.

Chapter Two

Over the opponent's all fours

As you can see from the accompanying illustrations you are in a pretty favourable position here to get back to your feet and run or finish from the vertical posture while the opponent is still on the floor. When this is an option I think you should take it. Having said that the opponent may be a dangerous vertical fighter that you do not want to allow back to his feet (just because you are up and he is down is no guarantee of your victory). All said and done the option is yours. At one of my recent seminars a guy said to me, 'surely you don't want to be on the floor in that position, why don't you just get back up again?'

Oh if only it were always that simple, as I have said in many other books you very rarely have the choice of getting back to your feet because your opponent will not just let you get back up again because he knows how vulnerable he is going to be if you're up and he's down. He'll grip onto anything and everything for dear life to keep you on the floor with him, as

Fighting From Your Knees

will you if you are in the same position. Whilst there is a choice you may way up the pros and cons and take that choice, when there isn't you have to make the best of fighting from where you are. Again, by denying that there will be times when the opponents will not allow you to get back up you will not address the problem, so accept it and deal with it. More often than not you will not have the option to get back to your feet and you are going to have to fight from the ground or get battered for your ignorance.

This is actually a very strong position to find yourself in. If you know what to do with it, it offers many good finishing techniques or possibilities of moving to stronger positions.

To defend the hold simply sprawl your legs back straight and as far as you can, this will break the opponent's grip on your legs and enable you to spread your weight and make it hard for him to escape. To finish from here takes practised technique, also, many people have lost the fight from this controlling position when they have moved to finish, so make sure that your finishers are polished.

Reverse naked choke

Feed your right arm under the opponent's chin and across his throat so the bone of your wrist is along and into his wind pipe. Couple at the other side with your left hand to make the choke. Lift and force your right wrist into his throat.

Shoulder base choke

If it is not possible to couple the right and left hand to make the choke, very often it will not be, then feed your right arm right under and out the other side. Place your left palm on the opponent's back or shoulder and then grab your own left biceps with your right hand and squeeze your arms and chest together, this will finish the choke.

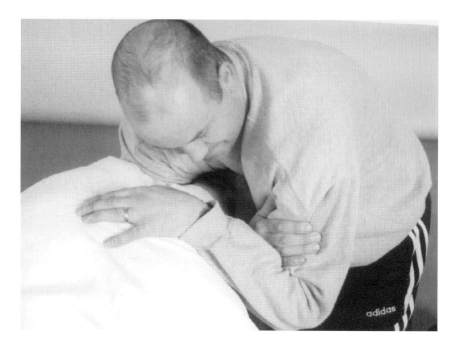

Turn over

Feed your right arm under the opponent's left arm-pit and force him over onto his back and take up the mount position.

Fighting From Your Knees

Sit through to arm/shoulder bar

Grab the opponent's inside left wrist with your right hand, sit your left leg through from your left to your right, as you do so fall across the opponent's left arm by placing your left arm-pit over his shoulder and pulling his arm up straight to bar the elbow and/or shoulder, as per illustration.

Ankle grab and turn

Reach behind the opponent with your right arm and grab his left ankle, lift his foot and knee off the floor and pull/push him over to your left hand side and onto his back. From here take any strong hold that is available, probably side 4 1/4, the mount or the scarf hold.

Fighting From Your Knees

Juji Gatame

Feed your right arm under the opponent's left arm-pit and force him over onto his back, as he turns place your right foot at the far side of his head and at the same time bring your left leg by the left side of his body, keep control of his right arm. Lie onto your back and trap the opponent's head with your right leg, simultaneously wedge your right foot underneath his body at his left hand side. His arm is between your legs, pull down on his arm and push up with your hips to complete the bar.

This is quite a difficult position to take the arm bar from. Much practice will be needed to make it smooth; once you have the technique however you will catch many opponents.

Sit through and triangular leg choke

Force the opponent's head between your legs, step up with your left leg and feed your right arm under his arm-pit, as you pull him over to your left hand side turn to your own right and sit it down. Hook your right leg around his neck and pull him backwards so that he is now lying on his back and you are sitting up with your leg still around his neck. Wrap your right foot around the back of your left knee and squeeze your thighs tightly to make the choke.

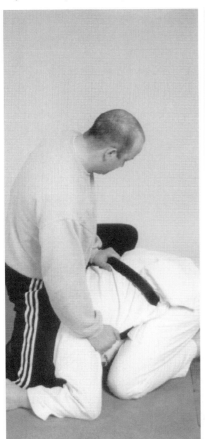

Fighting From Your Knees

Turn and face bar/choke

Move around to the opponent's right side (or left) simultaneously feeding your right arm under his chin (if going for the face bar feed your right arm across his face so that the bone of the wrist is across his cheek bone, teeth, nose, or eye). Pull him backwards so that he falls between your legs and into your scissor guard. At the same time join your right and left hand to make the choke. As you squeeze your arms to make the choke push down with your feet and stretch the opponent, this will better secure and tighten the hold.

Over the opponent's all fours

Turn and lapel choke

Grab the opponent's left collar with your right hand, move around to his right hand side feeding your right arm under his throat, pull the lapel tightly to make the choke. If you need more leverage reach over with your left arm and grab his left arm under the elbow and pull him back towards you. As you do so hook your left leg over his left arm and tie it off, pull hard with your right arm to tighten the lapel around his throat to make the choke.

Over the opponent's all fours

Elbow strike to arm bar

If the opponent has wrapped his arms around your right leg lift up your right elbow and strike him in the back, between the shoulder blades. As he reacts to the pain shoot your right leg underneath and sit through, as illus, this will force his right arm up, drop your right arm-pit onto his shoulder and lift his arm up to make the bar.

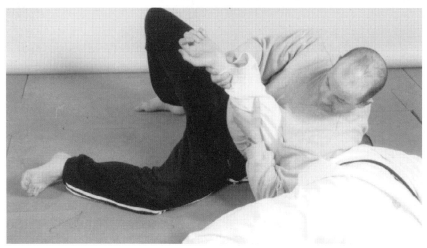

Leg grab to face bar

As the opponent grabs your right leg step slightly to his right with your left leg, feed your right arm across his face and couple at the otherside with your left hand to make the face bar. If you need to you can force the opponent backwards with the bar into your scissor guard. The face bar is one of the most painful holds in the book and the illustrations will not do it justice, you have to feel it to believe it.

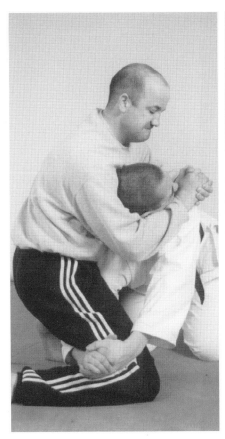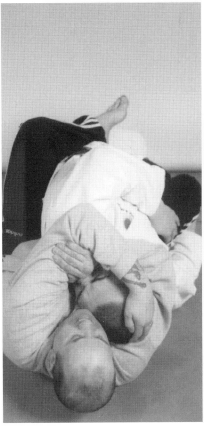

Fighting From Your Knees

You can also use your knees to attack the opponent from this position though there is not a great deal of potency in the attack, as a good defensive measure I always grab the opponent's sleeves or arms to disable them for his own defence or attack.

As with everything else make up your own techniques and improvise, nothing is cast in stone. Most of my favourite techniques are variations on old themes or techniques that I have just found myself.

Chapter Three

Under the opponent's all fours

This is indeed a vulnerable position to be in, and one that seems to occur quite often. As with most susceptible positions on the floor the sooner you escape the better.

You may take a little solace from the fact that although it is not a good position to be in, over the all fours, which is where the opponent is when you are under them, it is not a very strong position for the inexperienced opponent either. He will most likely try to stand up, leaving himself vulnerable to leg throws.

Having said that you do need escapes and finishes from every position.

Immediate sit through

The best time to escape is immediately, before the opponent has a chance to secure his hold.

As soon as you find yourself under the opponent's all fours, sit through with your right leg and arc your back across his.

Then very quickly turn and catch the opponent before he has a chance to readjust (hard to explain - look at the pics).

Elbow hook

If the opponent has his arms around your waist, he very often will have, reach up with your right arm and hook it around his elbow, nice and tightly. Then quickly sit through with your right leg towards your own left hand side and, as the opponent falls forward mount him from the back.

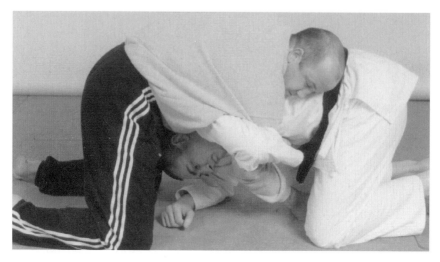

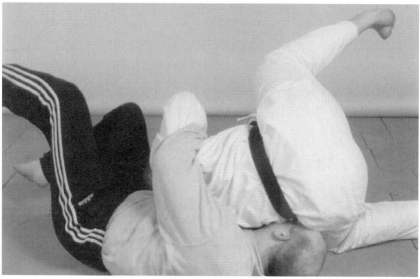

Alternatively you can hook the elbow in the same way and sit through with your left leg to your own right handside. This will leave you with your back on your opponent's chest, lean heavily on him and then place your right arm around his neck and take the scarf hold position or roll over the opponent and take the side 4 1/4 hold down.

Fighting From Your Knees

Hug turn

If the opponent has his arms around your stomach and is hugging very tightly you can turn him without securing one of his arms. Simply sit through, either side, and roll over as though rolling onto your back, this will bring the opponent with you and he will end up on his back with your back across his chest. From here keep your weight firmly pinned on him until your can break his grip and roll in to the side 4 1/4. If his grip is tight bend his little finger or thumb (or any finger that is open to attack) until he releases his grip.

Groin grab

It's an oldy but a goody, what I always say is if all else fails grab him by the ****ocks, whilst it will be difficult to finish from here he will definitely move enabling an escape. As he reacts to the pain quickly turn him onto his back.

Pressure point turn

Press, or punch, the pressure point in the middle of the thigh and force the opponent over onto his back. This is a rainy day technique that is worth knowing for the one or two times that it might work. Some people react really well to this technique others not at all, but when it does work it gets you out of the shit, which is good enough.

While you are in this position you will have the chance, at one time or another to try them all.

Chapter four

At the opponent's side

Another strong position to be in, that offers both the chance to stand and finish from the vertical position and the chance to finish with a myriad of good techniques. This the position that many experienced ground fighters love to be in because there is little chance of escape for the inexperienced fighter who will usually try to stand up and fall victim immediately to a punishing choke hold.

If the option is there you may wish to stand up and either run away or finish the opponent whilst he is still on his knees - the choice, as they say, is yours. If this were a self defence situation I'd say get up and run at the very earliest opportunity, if it is a fight situation there may be contributing factors that you need to look at.

In one of my many street altercations I have been faced with this choice - the guy I was fighting was a hardened street fighter with the hands of a pro boxer. I felt that by standing back up again I might be giving him another shot at the title. I knew he was tough enough to take the few kicks that I could give him before he found his feet - on the other hand, though he felt strong on the floor I could feel his lack of ground fighting experience and panic, his punching prowess on the floor was about as useful as a jet ski on the M1. So I stayed on the floor, even though I could have got up, and knocked him out with a strangle, and when I say I knocked him out I mean I knocked him out - for a long time. When he woke up his fight had completely gone, he was just happy to be alive and wanted to buy me a drink.

Had I stood back up and allowed this guy his arena - who knows? So at the opponent's side is a good controlling place to be.

I think it is worth mentioning at this point that, against the Judoka, in the controlled arena where atemi may not be permissible, it is very hard to finish from this position. Judo players are expert at defending from the 'hedgehog' position- but that is slightly out of the context of this book about making it work where there are no rules.

Fighting From Your Knees

Face bar/choke

Usually my first line attack from this position would be the face bar or choke. Stay on your right knee and straighten your left leg behind and along the opponent's body so that when you take the bar or choke the opponent will fall into your scissor guard where you can control him better. Feed your right arm under his chin (if going for the face bar feed your right arm across his face so that the bone of the wrist is across his cheek bone, teeth, nose, or eye). Pull him backwards so that he falls between your legs and into your scissor guard, at the same time join your right and left hand to make the choke (or alternatively grab your left biceps with your right and wrap your left hand behind the opponent's head to make a hugging choke).

As you squeeze your arms to make the choke push down with your feet and stretch the opponent, this will better secure and tighten the hold. If the opponent resists halfway bite his ear or face to distract him so that you can finish the move.

Lapel choke

Feed your right arm under the opponent's chin, from your right to your left, and grab his far lapel or collar and pull it back so that it tightens across his throat to make the choke/ strangle.

If you are struggling with the leverage reach over with your left arm and grab his left arm under the elbow and pull him back towards you. As you do so hook your left leg over his left arm and tie it off, pull hard with your right arm to tighten the lapel around his throat to make the choke.

Fighting From Your Knees

Juji Gatame

Feed your right arm over the opponent's back and under his left armpit and pull him, back towards you and over onto his back, as he turns place your right foot at the far side of his head and at the same time bring your left leg by the left side of his body, keep control of his right arm. Lie onto your back and trap the opponent's head with your right leg, simultaneously wedge your right foot underneath his body at his left hand side. His arm is between your legs, pull down on his arm and push up with your hips to complete the bar. This is quite a difficult position to take the arm bar from. Much practise will be needed to make it smooth, once you have the technique however you will catch many opponents.

Arm grab to back

Feed your right arm across the opponent's face, from your right to your left, and grab around the front, of his upper left arm.

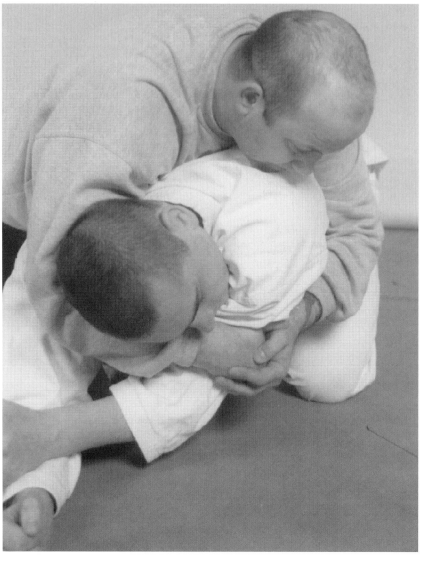

Feed your left arm under the opponent's body and grab the back of his left upper arm. Pull with both hands so that his arm comes off the floor, push with your chest so that he topples over onto his back, take up the side 4 1/4 hold down.

Fighting From Your Knees

Foot turn

Grab the opponent's right foot with your left hand, lift it off the floor and topple him forward onto his back, take up the side 4 1/4 or the mount.

Foot and arm turn

Feed your right arm across the opponent's face, from your right to your left, and grab around the front of his upper left arm. At the same time grab the opponent's right foot with your left hand, lift it off the floor. Pull his arm and lift his foot simultaneously to topple him forward onto his back, take up the side 4 1/4 or the mount.

Mounted Juji Gatame

Sit on top of the opponent's back, grab under his left arm with your right arm and then slip over to his left hand side and onto your left shoulder. Force your right foot under the opponent's chin hooking and scraping it backwards until the opponent falls to his left and onto his back - keep a good grip on his arm. Lie onto your back and trap the opponent's head with your right and left leg, as illus. His arm is between your legs, pull down on his arm and push up with your hips to complete the bar.

This is an advanced form of Juji Gatame, much practise will be needed to make it smooth, once you have the technique however you will catch many opponents.

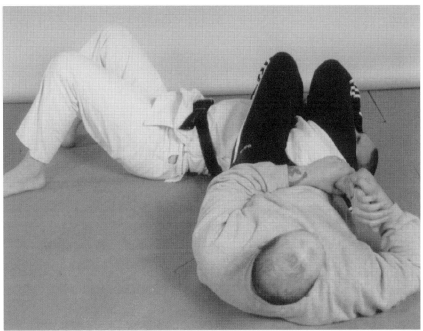

Fighting From Your Knees

Belt grab and Juji Gatame

Sit on top of the opponent's back, facing forwards. Taking your right leg out of the mount, turn and face the opposite way to the opponent. At the same time grab his belt (or the top of his trousers) with your left hand (make sure that your left foot is tucked neatly between his thighs) and hook under his left arm with your right. Sit backwards forcefully and at the same time pull on the opponent's belt and sweep upwards with your left leg to somersault the kneeling opponent forward and onto his back - keep a good grip of his left arm at all times. As he spins over, your legs will automatically be in the correct position for the bar.

Lie on your back and trap the opponent's head with your right and left leg, as illus. His arm is between your legs, pull down on his arm and push up with your hips to complete the bar.

Again, this is an advanced form of Juji Gatame and much practise will be needed to make it smooth.

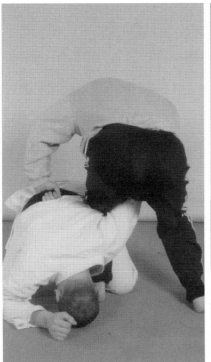
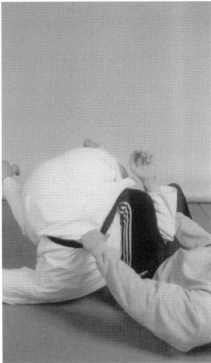

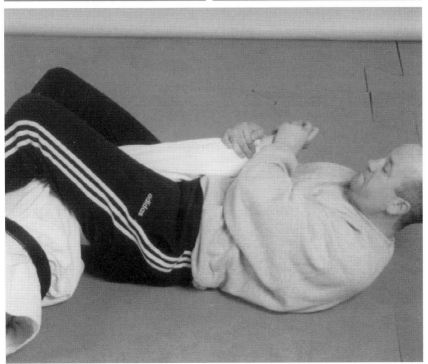

Shoulder bar

Grab the opponent's right wrist with your right hand and pull it outwards and from under him, simultaneously throw your right arm over his arm so that your arm-pit sits across his shoulder, force him to the ground by sitting through with your left leg and dropping your weight on his shoulder. Force his right arm up and straight with your right hand to complete the bar.

Lip turn and choke

Reach over the opponent's head with your left hand and grab a finger into the very corner of his mouth, being very careful not to go to close to his teeth. Wrench his head back towards you, as it does so wrap your right arm around his throat, as illus, and couple up with your left to make the choke. Pull the opponent into your scissor guard to finish the move.

Fighting From Your Knees

Chapter Five

Drilling

As with all the other volumes of this text the drilling is the imperative chapter that cannot be ignored if excellence is your goal. If you just look at the pictures and expect it to miraculously happen then you're in for a big shock when reality hits you in the eye like a ball pin hammer. Even the best techniques in the world fail if they are not tempered on the controlled arena, the great Sumo wrestlers in Japan have a saying 'cry in the gym, laugh in the ring'.

The great Bing Crosby, a legendary dancer in his day would wear out a new pair of shoes to perfect one dance step, the jugglers of the old circus days would juggle until their hands bled and golfing greats spend hour upon hour working on only one putt in a bid to make it theirs.

They are all unique in one way - they put years of flight time into hours of practise. In the old Bubokan days the instructors

Fighting From Your Knees

would limit their fighters to certain technique for up to six months, not allowing them to use their favourite contest winning technique. For six months they would lose nearly all their fights in a bid to perfect a new technique and have to suffer the ridicule of people saying that they were not so good without their favourite throw. Throughout history all the greats drilled from morn till night in a bid to be perfect at a technique and find that elusive 'feel'.

If you only half practise a technique then you will only half get it and be half as good as you could be, so dig in and get some flight time under your belt.

The following drills are only my suggestions, they are drills that I personally favour, try these and then make up your own so that you can learn to flow with the different techniques, eventually allowing them to flow into each other.

Note:

For more detail on the techniques involved in the drills refer to relevant chapter and illustrations.

Snatch and turn

Snatch the opponent down and quickly move to his left side. Snatch and turn 20 times and then do the same to his right hand side. It's very important that you do these moves left and right so that you can manipulate an opponent from all sides and angles.

Arm Drag

Elbow the opponent with your right elbow and drop your arm-pit and body weight onto his right arm, drag him to the floor and then go back to the start position - 20 reps each side.

Knee trap

Trap the opponent's right knee with your left foot, sit back and pull him to his back and roll into the mount, return to the start position - repeat 20 times both sides.

Fighting From Your Knees

Head lock and turn

Grab the opponent in a right head lock and pull him onto his back, return to the start position and do the same to the left, 40 reps in all.

Broken choke

Duck under the opponent's right arm and choke him with your right arm, pull him down to the mount position - repeat 20 times each side.

Alternate turns

Kneeling over the opponent practise going to his right side and then his left as smoothly as possible.

Reverse naked choke

Practise the choke from left to right as fast and as smoothly as possible until they are equal - 100 reps each side.

Sprawling

Get the opponent to try and grab your legs, when he does sprawl them back as far and as straight as you can - 100 reps.

Immediate sit through

From under the opponent practise a fast sit through as soon as the opponent takes the hold, left and right for 30 reps each side.

Fast turning

Get the opponent to grip you very tightly around the waist and practise fast turns onto your back to the left and to the right.

As with everything practice until you are sick to death of the techniques and then they will be yours, if you don't you'll be sick to death of them failing for you when the shit hits the fan.

Conclusion

That is the end of the six volumes of ground fighting. I hope that you have enjoyed and learned from them. The books are not exhaustive, and I am not the best grappler in the world, but the techniques within do and have worked for me in situations where two men enter the arena and only one walks back out. I can't tell you about competing on the judo or wrestling mat because that is not my game. When rules are introduced I am not a skilful enough player in the physical syndrome to be a champion so I will not claim to be what I am not.

What I can tell you, however, is how it is on the pavement arena because I have been there enough times to call myself a veteran without fear of sounding pretentious. In that respect, which is the only respect that I can claim real expertise, my book will definitely prepare those perceptive enough to read with an honest and open mind.

Ground fighting is a well that never seems to run dry, the subject matter is so deep that it never ceases to amaze me, the deeper I have dug the deeper it has got - but that's what's so exciting about it. It's a journey with no end but lots of exciting stops. Just when you think you are getting there along comes a brilliant ground fighter like my friend Rick Young, or Neil Adams or the awe inspiring Gracies and you realise just how much more there is to learn. I have to say that I am still learning after 25 years in the martial arts and I can't see an end to it yet. I'm still as excited about the learning as I was as a spotty teenager with an eye on the Bruce Lee crown - me and a few million other would be's. Mr Lee was my idol and the reason I started the martial arts, and there's one thing of which I am very sure, if he were alive today ground fighting would be well and truly on his curriculum (actually it was already before he died, he trained with 'Judo' Gene La-bell, the famous American wrestler) along with all the other wonderful systems that there are today.

What we have to maintain is an open mind, not an open mind with tunnel vision like so many of the new wave martial artists that have found their own classical mess, but a true open mind where we accept other systems even if we personally do not rate them. There is more than one route to the peak

Fighting From Your Knees

of the mountain and no one ever reached that peak by denying that fact. I have made many friends from many system of the martial arts over the years all of whom I admire, and whilst many of them do not follow my way they have found ways of their own that run on a parallel.

I am aware that some people use books and videos as a safe place to find knowledge. Let me tell you here and now that in the world of martial arts there is no safe place of learning, if there is, if you think you have found one, then it is sure to be false, you cannot make an omelette without breaking a few eggs, just like you cannot be a boxer without getting a bloody nose.

So use these books and my videos to add to the knowledge that you are collating in your regular club or dojo, you can learn a lot from a book and a video, I have, but you cannot replace live training with the injection of that leveller we call fear. This is not to say that fear has to be present in the controlled arena at all times, rather it is to say that it should be injected at regular intervals otherwise what you are learning will mean very little, like learning to swim in an empty pool. Get immersed, get wet, get real - or join a ballet class.

Thank you once again for reading my book/s and remember to always be a nice person and temper ferocious fighting ability with kindness and compassion. If you never look for trouble then, when it seeks you out, justification will be your ally and there is no stronger ally than knowing that you are right.

If nothing else I hope this series has inspired you to join a good Judo or wrestling club.

Note:

For more on the art of ground fighting please refer to my ground fighting series of videos, volume 1-6 available by mail order.

For details visit www.geoffthompson.com.

Other books in this series:

GEOFF THOMPSON'S GROUND FIGHTING SERIES

PINS: THE BEDROCK

GROUND FIGHTING

GEOFF THOMPSON

SUMMERSDALE

GEOFF THOMPSON'S GROUND FIGHTING SERIES

THE ESCAPES

GROUND

GEOFF
THOMPSON

SUMMERSDALE

GEOFF THOMPSON'S GROUND FIGHTING SERIES

CHOKES AND STRANGLES

GEOFF THOMPSON

SUMMERSDALE

GEOFF THOMPSON'S GROUND FIGHTING SERIES

ARM BARS & JOINT LOCKS

GROUND FIGHTING

GEOFF THOMPSON

SUMMERSDALE

GEOFF THOMPSON'S GROUND FIGHTING SERIES

FIGHTING FROM YOUR BACK

GEOFF THOMPSON

SUMMERSDALE

www.geoffthompson.com

www.summersdale.com